Story & Art by
Miyoshi Tomori

Volume 3

A Devil and Her Love Song

Volume 3

CONTENTS

STORY THUS FAR

Maria's forthright nature inspires Tomoyo Kohsaka to start being true to herself, and after seeing the two of them come to school together and stand up to their classmates, Yusuke Kanda begins to change too.

When Maria is forced to become the choir leader for the upcoming school choral competition, the class revolts and refuses to attend rehearsals. Meanwhile, a girl who has been out sick for weeks is about to return…

A Devil and Her Love Song
Song 14

OKAY, SCHOOL'S OVER!
TOMOYO KOHSAKA! SHIN MEGURO! READY FOR SOME FUN? IT'S REHEARSAL TIME!
BIIING
BOOOONG
BIIING
...
OH... UM...
BUT YUSUKE ISN'T HERE...
Ha ha...

IF YUSUKE KANDA ISN'T INTERESTED—
"ISN'T INTER-ESTED" IN WHAT?
DON'T SHUT ME OUT.
I WAS JUST DOWN THE HALL.
I TALKED TO THE OTHER GUYS.
THEY SAY THEY DON'T MIND PARTICI-PATING.
THEY'RE WAITING BY THE MUSIC ROOM.
THAT'S ALL.

SO YOU'RE SAYING YOU TALKED THEM INTO IT?
HUH ?!
YOU GAVE THEM ONE OF YOUR HEARTFELT SPEECHES?
WHAT?
AND YOU WON THEM OVER. IS THAT IT?
AH...
CONGRATS. YOU WANTED TO BE MR. POPULAR, AND NOW YOU ARE.
SHIN—!
I'm going ahead.
IT WASN'T LIKE THAT.
I-I DIDN'T...

SO EASILY EMBARRASSED BY THE TRUTH?
YOU'RE FORGETTING YOUR LOVELY SPIN.
Oooh!
YOU'RE TEASING ME, MARIA!
flinch
?!
OH... SORRY.
I WAS JUST GONNA MAKE THE FISH FACE.
SCRUNCH
FISH FACE! ♡
"FISH FACE"?

YOU LOOK UTTERLY RIDICU- LOUS.
HEY, MARIA...
I'LL GO TALK TO THE TEACHER.
TURN
WE NEED THE MUSIC ROOM KEY.
YOU'RE FORGETTING YOUR LOVELY SPIN TOO...
THE KEY?

YOU SAID YOU DIDN'T NEED MY HELP.
SO NOW WHAT?
I'D INTENDED TO PRACTICE IN THE CLASS-ROOM.
BUT WE HAVE AN ACCOMPANIST NOW...
...AND HALF OF THE CLASS IS WILLING TO PARTICIPATE.
I'M SORRY TO TROUBLE YOU...
...BUT I'D LIKE TO USE THE PIANO IN THE MUSIC ROOM.
PLEASE, SIR.
WELL, THAT'S TOO BAD.
SOBA BORO

YOU SAID YOU DIDN'T NEED MY HELP.
YOU NEED TO STAND BEHIND YOUR WORDS.
WHAT?
WE CAN'T USE THE MUSIC ROOM?!
IF YOU DON'T NEED AN ACCOM-PANIST, I'M OFF.
IS THAT RELIEF I HEAR, SHIN?
DID ALL THESE PEOPLE MAKE YOU PANIC?
I know you hate playing for an audience.
I'M SORRY.
WHAT KIND OF LEADER ARE YOU?
DON'T WASTE OUR TIME.
WHAM
Meep!
Shin? An accom-panist?
MUR-MUR
UM...

THERE'S AN ORGAN IN OUR CLUB STORAGE ROOM.
YOU COULD PROBABLY USE IT.
WAY TO GO, ORCHESTRA CLUB!
THAT BOOKLET OF MARIA'S WAS INTEREST-ING...
HOW'RE WE GONNA CARRY IT, YUSUKE?
ON OUR SHOULDERS! WE'LL TAKE TURNS.
CAN WE BRING THE ORGAN TO THE CLASS-ROOM?
ARE YOU SERIOUS?

ALL THOSE STUDENTS GATHERING TOGETHER FOR HER...
IT'LL GO STRAIGHT TO HER HEAD.
"HER" WHO?
I'M SORRY I'VE BEEN OUT FOR SO LONG! HERE'S MY DOCTOR'S NOTE.
I came straight from the hospital.

HANA! YOU'RE FEELING BETTER?
I'M TOTALLY FINE!
I'LL BE BACK IN CLASS TOMORROW.
OH, WOW!
WHAT A GORGEOUS PENDANT!
SOBA
YOU LIKE THAT KIND OF THING?
OF COURSE I DO! IT'S SO COOL! GOOD QUALITY, TOO. IT LOOKS SO AUTHENTIC!
And it's real silver!
TAKE IT. IT'S YOURS.
WHAT?
B-BUT... ARE YOU SURE? IT LOOKS EXPENSIVE...
OF COURSE I'M SURE.

YOU SHOULD WEAR IT TOMORROW.
PEEK
MORNING...

HANA?!
IT'S HANA! NO WAY!
YOU WERE DIS-CHARGED FROM THE HOSPITAL?
IT'S BEEN AGES!
THAT'S GREAT! WE MISSED YOU.
LONG TIME NO SEE. HOW LONG HAS IT BEEN?
A LITTLE OVER TWO WEEKS?
WE REALLY MISSED YOU.
TEARY

WAAH
I LOVE YOU GUYS!
I MISSED YOU ALL SO MUCH!
GLOMP
DON'T CRY, HANA.
BUT I... I'M SO HAPPY.
I WAS SCARED I WOULDN'T BE WELCOMED BACK.
EVERYONE LOVES HAVING YOU AROUND.
SNIFFLE
LIKE THAT'D HAPPEN.
YOU'RE SO ADORABLE.

WHO ARE YOU?
OH, HER. SHE'S NEW.
SHE GOT HERE THE DAY AFTER YOU LEFT.
REALLY? WOW, YOU'RE BEAUTIFUL!
THAT'S "DEVIL MARIA."
I'M MARIA KAWAI, ACTUALLY.
UM ...
UH ...

Beam
I'M HANA IBUKI!
JUST CALL ME "HANA."
OH.
I'M SORRY!
CLAP
BOW
ARE YOU MAD AT ME?
YOU LOOK MAD...
DID I DO SOMETHING WRONG?
DON'T MIND HER!
THAT'S HOW SHE ALWAYS LOOKS.

UH... NO.
IT'S JUST THAT CROSS YOU'RE—
MORNING, MARIA!
YUSUKE!
GET THIS! THIS GUY HERE PRACTICED SO MUCH...
...THAT HIS VOICE IS ALL SCRATCHY.
WE'RE PRACTICING AFTER SCHOOL AGAIN, RIGHT?
I BROUGHT SOME LOZENGES.

HANA...?
WHEN I WAS MEMORIZING NAMES FROM THE CLASS DIRECTORY...
...I NOTICED THERE WAS SOMEONE MISSING.
BIIING
BOOONG
BIIING
ALL THE GIRLS SEEM QUITE FOND OF HER.
YEP, THAT'S HANA.

SHE'S A NICE GIRL.
WHEN YUSUKE KANDA SAID THAT...
...WHY DID HIS SMILE LOOK SO FORCED?
HANA, ABOUT THAT CROSS...
IT WAS AS IF HIS LOVELY SPIN WENT RIGHT OUT THE WINDOW.
ISN'T IT GREAT? THE TEACHER GAVE IT TO ME.
YOU'D BETTER KEEP QUIET ABOUT IT.

TUG
WHAT DO YOU MEAN, AYU...?
WATCH OUT FOR THAT MARIA KAWAI!
SHE WAS EXPELLED FROM HER OLD SCHOOL!
OUR TEACHER HAS IT IN FOR HER TOO.
BUT HE JUST LOVES YOU.
IF SHE FINDS OUT HE GAVE IT TO YOU, SHE COULD DO ANYTHING!
...
HANA IBUKI.

HERE'S THE BOOKLET FOR THE COMPETITION.
Chor Competition Booklet Amazing Grace
WE'RE GOING TO REHEARSE NOW. I HOPE YOU'LL PARTICIPATE.
HEY, BOSS LADY. I'M CLEARING THE TABLES.
IT'S SO LIGHT.
BETCHA IT'S EMPTY.
WHOSE STUPID DESK IS THIS?
MINE! GOT A PROBLEM?
SHIN WAS REALLY GOOD YESTERDAY.
YEAH. SCARY GOOD.
...
KLAT
MARIA, HOW DO YOU PRONOUNCE THIS?
OH, THAT'S—

COME ON, HANA! LET'S GO!
HANA?
THIS ISN'T RIGHT...

THIS IS ALL WRONG!
WHY...
...IS THE CLASS DIVIDED THIS WAY?

WE SHOULD BE DOING THIS TOGETHER!
C'MON, EVERY-ONE!
AND YOU GUYS! LEAVING THE GIRLS OUT? THAT'S MEAN!
You should ask them to join in.
WE DIDN'T MEAN TO.

Come on!
WE DIDN'T TELL THEM NOT TO SING!
IT JUST... HAPPENED ...
JUST LIKE THAT...
...SHE DID WHAT I COULDN'T DO. SHE DID IT SO EASILY...
SHE WAS LIKE AN ANGEL.
AS IF SHE'S THE EXACT OPPOSITE OF ME.

A Devil and Her Love Song

A Devil and Her Love Song
Song 15

SORRY ABOUT YESTERDAY, MARIA!

I FEEL LIKE MAYBE I STEPPED ON YOUR TOES.
YOU'RE THE LEADER OF OUR GROUP, RIGHT? I DIDN'T MEAN TO MAKE YOU LOOK BAD...
BUT... BUT I COULDN'T JUST LEAVE THINGS LIKE THAT.
AYU AND THE OTHER GIRLS LOOKED SO SAD.
I SPOKE UP WITHOUT THINKING.
I'M NOT CRITICIZING THE WAY YOU'RE HANDLING THINGS, I SWEAR—

NO, I'M GLAD YOU SAID WHAT YOU DID.
THE CLASS WAS DIVIDED. NOW EVERYONE'S TOGETHER, THANKS TO YOU.
I'M NOT DEAD SET ON DOING THINGS MY WAY.
IN FACT, I'M GRATEFUL TO YOU.
THANKS.

IT WAS NO BIG DEAL!
DON'T FEEL BAD ABOUT IT, MARIA! OKAY?
SHE SAYS SUCH KIND THINGS.
Don't talk to Devil Maria!
AND SHE SEEMS SINCERE.

SO WHY DO I FEEL SO UNEASY ...?
HANA? I HAVEN'T TALKED TO HER ALL THAT MUCH.
I barely know her.
SO YOU'RE NOT ONE OF THE "OTHER GIRLS" SHE WAS TALKING ABOUT.
SHE DIDN'T COUNT YOU.
Warm up in pairs!
UM...
That's not nice!
WELL, SHE NEVER BULLIED ME OR ANYTHING.
BY THE WAY, ARE YOU GOING TO PAIR UP WITH ME?
I USUALLY WARM UP ALONE...
YOU CAN DO IT ALONE?
HEADS UP!

BAM!
SORRY! ARE YOU OKAY?!
I THREW IT TOO HARD...
MARIA ...!
TREMBLE
TREMBLE
No control at all...
My hand's gone numb. Gosh, I wonder why?
Eek! She's pissed!
MUTTER
SORRY, SORRY!
LET ME TAKE A LOOK.
OH!

YOU'RE HURT—!
I'M SORRY!
I—
OW... IT REALLY HURTS, AND IT'S ALL YOUR FAULT.
YOU SHOULD SEE THE NURSE.
I HAVE TO ICE IT. NO MORE P.E. FOR ME.
MARIA...
YOU DIDN'T GET THIS INJURY FROM THE BALL.
...
ISN'T THIS CUT FROM WHEN YOU GRABBED YOUR CROSS?
...

TOOK YOU LONG ENOUGH.
YOU'RE SO SLOW.
YOU'RE EMBARRASSED TOO.
YOU KNOW HOW MUCH I HATE IT WHEN PEOPLE INSIST THEY'RE FINE WHEN THEY'RE REALLY NOT.
YOU FAKED BEING MAD TO MAKE ME FEEL BETTER.
YOUR LOVELY SPIN IS HARD TO UNDERSTAND SOMETIMES.
THAT WASN'T MY INTENTION.
NOW STOP BEING STUBBORN! YOUR HAND'S ALL RED!

YUSUKE, YOU STAY HERE.
LET'S GO TAKE CARE OF THAT, MARIA.
SPLOOSH
YUSUKE AND I ARE CHILDHOOD FRIENDS.
MY FAMILY BELONGS TO HIS TEMPLE. WE'VE VISITED GRAVES TOGETHER SINCE WE WERE LITTLE.
BUT IT'S NOT LIKE WE'RE BEST FRIENDS OR ANYTHING.

IS THAT A RELIEF?
KYU
I THINK YOU HAVE THE WRONG IDEA.
THERE'S NOTHING BETWEEN YUSUKE KANDA AND ME.
BUT HOW DO YOU FEEL ABOUT HIM?
HE'S A NICE GUY.

OH! IS THAT ALL?
I HATE LYING, SO I'LL JUST TELL YOU.
I'VE PRETTY MUCH HAD A CRUSH ON HIM MY WHOLE LIFE!
BUT HE DOESN'T TAKE ME SERIOUSLY.
IN FACT, ALL THE BOYS IN CLASS TREAT ME LIKE ONE OF THEM.
I GUESS I'M NOT SEXY LIKE YOU.

WHAT ANSWER ARE YOU LOOKING FOR?
ARE YOU TELLING ME TO STAY AWAY FROM HIM?
WHAT ...? THAT SOUNDS LIKE I'M THREATENING YOU.
WHY ELSE WOULD YOU SAY THAT OUT OF THE BLUE?
WHAT DO YOU MEAN?
IT'S JUST NORMAL GIRL TALK!
DON'T YOU TALK TO YOUR FRIENDS ABOUT THIS STUFF?
TELL EACH OTHER WHO YOU LIKE?

ALL FRIENDS TALK THIS WAY!
I DON'T REALLY...
...LIKE ANYONE IN PARTI-CULAR.
I'VE NEVER FALLEN IN LOVE OR TALKED TO ANYONE ABOUT IT.
HAS ANYONE SAID THEY LIKE YOU?
NO.
YOU'RE KIDDING!
NO, I'M NOT.
I'VE BEEN HATED AND SHUNNED, THOUGH.
PFFT

YOU'VE REALLY GOT TO FALL IN LOVE, MARIA!
IT'LL IMPROVE YOUR ATTITUDE.
I COULD INTRODUCE YOU TO SOMEONE—
WILL YOU SHUT UP...?
STOP BABBLING ABOUT STUPID STUFF LIKE THAT. I CAN'T SLEEP.
OH...
TWITCH

ST-STUPID STUFF ...?
Did you really just say that?
TURN
SHIN, YOU'RE IN LOVE WITH MARIA! RIGHT?
HMM. THAT WAS IMPECCABLE TIMING!
I SEE HOW IT IS!
...
Speechless
THE CONVERSATION TAKES AN ODD TURN.
Eeee!
HE SPOKE UP THE SECOND I SAID I'D SET YOU UP WITH SOMEONE.
Eeee!
SEE, MARIA? YOU DO HAVE SOMEBODY TO LOVE!
DON'T WORRY, I WON'T TELL ANYBODY!
Take your time. I'll leave you two alone.

IS SHE RIGHT, DELINQUENT?
...
SHE MOST CERTAINLY IS NOT.
YOU DON'T HAVE TO BE THAT EMPHATIC.
AND HERE I WAS THINKING I MIGHT TRY FALLING IN LOVE.
YOU RUINED THE MOMENT.
THAT'S TOTALLY BACKWARD.

YOU DON'T TRY TO FALL IN LOVE.
YOU JUST FALL.
I PITY WHO-EVER...
...FALLS IN LOVE WITH A GIRL LIKE YOU.

"YOU JUST FALL" ...
HEY, HANA.
YES?
THAT CROSS YOU'RE WEARING...
IS IT REALLY YOURS?
HUH? WHY DO YOU ASK?
OF COURSE IT'S MINE. CUTE, ISN'T IT?

IT LOOKS JUST LIKE ONE MARIA HAS.
I DON'T KNOW ANYTHING ABOUT IT.
I THINK IT'S MARIA'S—
SORRY IF I'M WRONG.
BUT IF IT'S NOT YOURS, WILL YOU GIVE IT BACK?
ARE YOU ACCUSING ME OF SOMETHING?
TEARY
THAT'S NOT WHAT I'M SAYING.
OKAY...

WHY IS EVERYONE ACTING LIKE I DID SOMETHING WRONG?
I NEVER SAID YOU...
NO, I'M SORRY.
CRYING LIKE THIS ISN'T FAIR.
IT JUST MADE ME KIND OF SAD...
...THAT YOU DIDN'T HAVE MORE FAITH IN ME.
I GET IT, YUSUKE. I DO.
I'LL GIVE IT BACK TO MARIA AFTER REHEARSAL.

AFTER ALL, WE'RE FRIENDS.
Choral Competition Booklet Amazing Grace
WELL...
Well, well, well...
Chatter Chatter
BUT IT IS BETTER WHEN EVERY-ONE'S INVOLVED.
HANA...! ♡
GIRLS SURE DO MAKE A DIFFERENCE.
THE SOUND'S A LOT RICHER NOW.
LIKE HE KNOWS ABOUT MUSIC.
Ha ha ha

TOMOYO KOHSAKA.
HUH?
DO YOU LIKE ANYONE?
I DON'T.
WHAT'RE YOU GUYS TALKING ABOUT?
OH!
I spoke too loud...
WHO DOESN'T LIKE ANYBODY?
Um...
I think it's perfectly fine not to like anyone! Ha...ha ha.
What should I say?
SHIVER
SHIVER
...

SHE LIKES TO LEAD THEM ON...
...SO SHE CAN TURN THEM DOWN IN FRONT OF EVERYONE. RIGHT, DEVIL MARIA?
BUT MARIA SAID NO ONE'S EVER TOLD HER THEY LIKE HER.
WELL, OBVIOUSLY IT WOULDN'T BE ANY FUN FOR HER.
ARE YOU REFERRING TO YUSUKE KANDA?
THAT WAS HARDLY A CONFESSION OF LOVE.
SEE? NOW SHE'S DENYING IT.
CALM DOWN. WHO CARES, ANYWAY?

LET'S JUST SAY SHE TURNED ME DOWN.
BUT THAT WOULD MAKE YOU—
MARIA.
YOU LIED TO ME?
YOU GOT ME TO POUR MY HEART OUT TO YOU!

HOW COULD YOU TRICK ME LIKE THAT?
I TRUSTED YOU!

A Devil and Her Love Song

A Devil and Her Love Song
Song 16

I TRUSTED YOU!
AND NOW IT TURNS OUT YOU BETRAYED ME.

BETRAYED YOU...?!
THAT WASN'T MY INTENTION.
EVERYTHING I SAID TO YOU IS TRUE.
BUT YUSUKE JUST SAID YOU TURNED HIM DOWN!
TELLING SOMEONE WHO YOU LIKE...
...IS PROOF OF FRIENDSHIP!
I TOLD YOU EVERYTHING. I TRUSTED YOU WITH MY FEELINGS!

AND YOU JUST WALKED ALL OVER THAT TRUST!
YOU'RE A HORRIBLE HUMAN BEING, MARIA!
HANA?
YOU SHOULD OWN UP TO WHAT YOU DID.
IF YOU KEEP BETRAYING YOUR FRIENDS LIKE THIS...
...YOU'LL BE MISERABLE.

DO YOU ENJOY PITYING PEOPLE?
WHAT ...?
THAT LOOK IN YOUR EYES REMINDS ME OF THE SISTERS...
SORRY, I GOT DISTRACTED. THERE'S BEEN A MISUNDER-STANDING.

YUSUKE KANDA AND I HAVE NO ROMANTIC INTEREST IN EACH OTHER.
YOU DON'T NEED TO WORRY.
BAFFLED
HUH ...?
HANA.
I HAVE NO IDEA WHAT YOU'RE TALKING ABOUT.
DON'T WORRY ABOUT WHAT?!
WHAT SHOULD I BE WORRIED ABOUT? YOU AND YUSUKE GETTING TOGETHER?
BUT EARLIER YOU ASKED ME—
THAT MAKES IT SOUND LIKE I WANT YUSUKE TO LIKE ME BACK...

...WHEN I'M HAPPY JUST TO FEEL THIS WAY ABOUT HIM!
HANA!
SLAM
WAIT, HANA—
DEVIL MARIA!
YOU'RE AWFUL!

TMP
SLAM
OPEN
TMP
TMP
TMP
THAT'S JUST GREAT.
AND HERE WE FINALLY HAD SOME PEACE AND QUIET...
MUTTER
MUTTER
DEFEATED
GIVE US A BREAK, MARIA.
Geez...
IT'S NOT MARIA'S FAULT.
I SHOULDN'T HAVE TRIED TO GLOSS OVER IT.
WHAT-EVER.
NOW THE GIRLS ARE MAD AGAIN.

AS I SAID, IT'S A MISUNDER-STANDING. I'LL TALK TO HER.
YOU WILL, WILL YOU?
JUST KEEP YOUR MOUTH SHUT!
You've done enough!
ARE YOU OKAY, MARIA?
NEVER MIND THAT NOW.
IT'S NONE OF MY BUSINESS, BUT SHOULDN'T YOU FOLLOW HER?
SHE JUST ANNOUNCED THAT SHE LIKES YOU.
OH, THAT? I ALREADY KNEW.
THE WHOLE CLASS KNOWS.

"JUST LIKING HIM MAKES ME HAPPY."
WE'VE HEARD IT A MILLION TIMES.
THE GIRLS TALK ABOUT IT IN CLASS.
We're done.
Let's go.
That killed the mood.
I ONLY JUST REALIZED...
...HOW HAPPY I WAS...

...THAT SHE CALLED ME A FRIEND.
"ALL FRIENDS TALK THIS WAY!"
BUT I WONDER WHAT SHE MEANS...
...BY "FRIEND"?
WE KNOW EXACTLY HOW YOU FEEL.
CHATTER
CHATTER
JUST IGNORE HER!
THE SIMPLE REALITY IS...

...PEOPLE DON'T SMILE AROUND ME...
...LIKE THEY DO AROUND HER.
You guys going home?
No sense staying.
For sure.
Ha ha ha
I KNEW IT.
SIGH

THIS IS BAD.
I'D BETTER PUT HANA IN CHARGE INSTEAD.
YOU MEAN HANA IBUKI?
SHE'S BACK IN CLASS?
YES, AND I'VE SEEN A CHANGE ALREADY.
IT'S A MUCH MORE CHEERFUL ENVIRONMENT.
blush

I KNEW MARIA KAWAI WASN'T FIT TO BE A LEADER.
LEADER, HUH?
Heh
...
I THINK...
...WE SHOULD KEEP MARIA IN THAT POSITION.
WHAT ARE YOU SAYING? HANA IS—
THE THING IS...

...A LOCAL TV STATION CALLED US.
THEY WANT TO TELEVISE A HIGH SCHOOL EVENT.
I SEE.
AT THIS POINT, WE'RE NOT SURE WE'RE GOING TO...
...MEET NEXT YEAR'S ENROLLMENT QUOTA.
WHY DON'T WE USE MARIA KAWAI FOR ADVERTISEMENT?

A DANGEROUS STUDENT GETS EXPELLED FROM THE PRESTIGIOUS ST. KATRIA...
...AND THROUGH OUR CHORAL COMPETITION, TOTSUKA HIGH REHABILITATES HER.
KRI...
OUR SLOGAN CAN BE...
..."A DEVIL CAN BECOME AN ANGEL...

...AT TOTSUKA HIGH SCHOOL."

OH...
I CAN SEE ST. KATRIA FROM HERE.
I MAY BE LACKING SOMETHING IMPORTANT.
SOME CRITICAL HUMAN ELEMENT LIKE WARMTH OR KINDNESS...
Amazing grace...
...OR THE ABILITY TO NOT OFFEND PEOPLE.
"YOU TAINT PEOPLE."
How sweet the sound...
THERE'S NO QUESTION THAT...
...hat saved a wretch...

...I LACK THE ABILITY TO MAKE PEOPLE HAPPY.
...like me...
SINGING BY YOURSELF AGAIN, MARIA?
I HEARD YOUR VOICE. I THOUGHT I'D FIND YOU HERE.
YOU WERE HERE ON YOUR FIRST DAY OF SCHOOL TOO.
DO YOU...

...SING WHEN YOU'RE SAD?

YEAH, AND WHEN SHE PANICS.

LIKE THAT TIME I GAVE YOU A PIGGY-BACK RIDE.

SHIN? WHAT'RE YOU DOING HERE?
AND WHAT ARE YOU DOING ...?
...Hiding behind the door?
TWITCH
AH... HA HA...

YOU'RE WORRIED ABOUT HER TOO, RIGHT?
WHY DON'T WE TRY TO USE THE MUSIC ROOM STARTING TOMORROW?
NO ONE USES IT EARLY IN THE MORNING.
REALLY?
YOU'VE COME A LONG WAY WITH THE CLASS.
I'M SURE THE TEACHER WILL RECONSIDER.
THERE'S NOTHING MORE I CAN DO.
NO...

MAYBE DOING NOTHING...
...IS THE BEST THING I CAN DO FOR THE CLASS.
WHAT ARE YOU TALKING ABOUT?
WHY ARE YOU SAYING THAT?
DON'T ...

DON'T BACK DOWN NOW...!
UP UNTIL NOW...
...I COULD RUN AWAY FROM ALL THE THINGS I HATED ABOUT MYSELF.
T... TOMOYO?
She's actually mad...?
GASP

BUT YOU CAME TO THIS SCHOOL...
...AND YOU MADE ME FACE THEM!
AND THAT MEANT...
...I HAD TO CHANGE!
HOW COULD I **NOT** CHANGE?
SO HOW CAN YOU SAY IT'S BETTER TO DO NOTHING?
OH...
ER...

SAME HERE.
YOU MADE ME REALIZE...
...THAT I'M NOT SUCH A LOSER AFTER ALL.
SOMETIMES YOUR HARSH COMMENTARY KILLS ME...
...BUT IT KIND OF FEELS GOOD—
OH!
BUT I'M NOT A MASOCHIST OR ANYTHING!
DON'T LOOK LIKE THAT!
MARIA...

A Devil and Her Love Song

A Devil and
Her Love Song
Song 17

I GRABBED HER AND
PULLED HER CLOSE...

THAT WAY, SHE'D HAVE
THE OPPORTUNITY TO CRY.

I COULDN'T THINK OF ANYTHING ELSE TO DO.
I WANTED TO COMFORT HER.
RUSTLE

YOU...
TH-THTHMP
GRAB
AH!
WHAT AM I DOING?
OH, CRAP...
I...
SHIN?
I HAVE TO SAY SOME-THING...
WHAT THE HECK IS WRONG WITH ME?!

I WANT TO COMFORT HER...
...BUT WHAT DOES SHE WANT?
I...
YOU...
STAY RIGHT WHERE YOU ARE!
I'M DOING WHAT I WANT.

WHOA, SHIN! BOLD MOVE!
TELLING HER TO STAY IN YOUR ARMS?
N-NO ...!
THAT'S NOT WHAT I MEANT.

WHAT I MEANT WAS...
...STAY HERE WITH US!
WHO CARES IF THE OTHERS DON'T LIKE YOU?
YOU'RE TOO HARSH FOR MOST PEOPLE.
IF EVERYONE LIKED YOU, THEY'D OBVIOUSLY BE FAKING IT!
...

And you, of course, are the soul of tact.
WHAT'S YOUR POINT?
WHAT GOOD WOULD LYING DO NOW?
MASH
...
THEY ALL HATE HER. THAT'S HOW IT IS!
SHAKE SHAKE
...
I-I suppose you're right. Ha...
I GUESS, BUT...
UM... MARIA...
RUMPLED
ARE YOU FINISHED YET?
YOU'RE ALL...

...SO FUNNY. HOW COULD I BE MAD?

ARE YOU SURE IT'S OKAY...
...FOR ME...
...TO STAY WITH YOU GUYS...?

HUG
OF COURSE IT'S OKAY.
HAVE SOME FAITH IN US.

YOU'RE A GOOD FRIEND.
THAT'S HOW WE REALLY FEEL.
AND TRY HAVING SOME FAITH IN YOURSELF TOO. YOU MADE THIS HAPPEN.

BELIEVE IN YOURSELF.
"BELIEVE IN YOURSELF."
IT SOUNDS SO MUCH BETTER...
...WHEN SOMEONE ELSE SAYS IT TO YOU.
WILL I...

...EVER BE ABLE TO RECIPROCATE?
Mor-ning!
Hi, Hana.
SNUB
...
HANA!
GOOD MORNING, SIR.
COME OVER HERE. I NEED TO TALK TO YOU.
GLANCE

MARIA!
I HEAR YOU'RE LEADING YOUR CLASS IN THE CHORAL COMPETITION.
WE'RE GOING TO BE ON TV!
TV...?
DO YOU KNOW THE VARIETY SHOW "TRAVELING ARROW"?
Haaah!
SPROING
Yokohama in Kanagawa Prefec-ture!
Let's go!
THEY SHOOT AN ARROW AT A MAP BLINDFOLDED, THEN VISIT A SCHOOL WHERE IT LANDS.
THEY HAVEN'T DONE IT YET, BUT...
SO THE ARROW HAS NOTHING TO DO WITH THE DECISION?
THAT'S THE REAL WORLD FOR YOU.
Ha ha ha
SO, MARIA...

I'M COUNTING ON YOU...
...TO CONTRIBUTE TO OUR SCHOOL.
WHAT ...?
WHAT DO YOU MEAN BY "CONTRIBUTE"?
SOUNDS LIKE YOU'RE USING STUDENTS FOR YOUR OWN AGENDA TO ME.
IN SOCIETY, YOU HAVE AN OBLIGATION TO CONTRIBUTE—
DON'T TWIST MY WORDS.

I DO WANT TO CONTRIBUTE.
I WANT TO DO SOMETHING FOR OTHERS.
BUT WHAT THAT "SOMETHING" **IS** IS UP TO ME.
LET'S BE CLEAR ABOUT THAT.
I'M NOT DOING THIS FOR YOU TEACHERS.
LET'S GO, SHIN.
UH... SURE.

EITHER WAY, THEY'RE VISITING US.
I GUESS IT'S A CHANCE TO PROMOTE THE SCHOOL.
TRY TO STAY CLEAR OF THE CAMERAS.
THEY'LL MANIPULATE THE FOOTAGE.
THEY CAN DO AS THEY PLEASE.
THEY MIGHT MAKE YOU LOOK AWFUL!
THE MEDIA SAY WHATEVER THEY WANT.
ARE YOU SPEAKING FROM EXPERI-ENCE?

SO THEY MADE A HUGE DEAL OUT OF MY PIANO DEBUT.
"LIKE FATHER, LIKE SON," YOU KNOW?
GULP
MY DAD...
HE'S A PRETTY WELL-KNOWN MUSICIAN.
THE PERFORMANCE SOLD OUT...
...BUT I GOT STAGE FRIGHT. IT WASN'T PRETTY.
I'VE BEEN A COWARD EVER SINCE.
THEY WERE PROBABLY ALL...
...GOSSIPING BEHIND MY BACK.

I DON'T WANT THAT TO HAPPEN TO YOU.
UH...
I MEAN...
YOU'VE BEEN FIGHTING THAT BATTLE ALL BY YOURSELF.
YOU'RE NO COWARD.
AND ANYWAY...
...

...I'M NOT ALONE.
NOT ANYMORE.
YOU ACT SO TOUGH.
CAN'T YOU EVER SAY "I'M COUNTING ON YOU"? IS THAT SO HARD?
IRKED

...I AM COUNTING ON YOU...
...TO DELIVER AN AMAZING PERFORMANCE ON TV.
You...! Salt in the wound, much?
"Devil" is right!
SHE DOESN'T EVEN REALIZE...
BI-I-I-NG
BO-O-O-NG
Time to rehearse.
...THAT SHE'S THE ONE WHO'S FIGHTING ALL BY HERSELF.
WE HAD A TALK AFTER SCHOOL YESTERDAY...
...ABOUT THE COMPETITION.

WHY DON'T YOU STEP DOWN?
LET'S BE FRANK. YOU CAN'T LEAD THIS CLASS.
IN FACT, YOU'RE THE ROOT OF THE PROBLEM.
MOST OF THE BOYS CAN'T BE BOTHERED.
NO ONE ASKED US...
AND ALL THE GIRLS AGREE WITH ME!
Huh ...?
STAY HOME ON THE DAY OF THE PERFOR-MANCE.
AND DON'T COME TO REHEARSALS, EITHER.

BUT I KNOW HOW HARD IT IS TO FIGHT ALL ALONE.

I WANT TO HELP HER.

I'VE GOT HER BACK, EVERY STEP OF THE WAY.

...IS WHAT...
...I WANT TO DO MOST.
mumble
AYU, YOU'RE HOPELESS.
WE'RE GOING TO BE ON TV!
WE ALL HAVE TO WORK TOGETHER...
...TO MAKE MARIA LOOK LIKE AN ANGEL.

A Devil and Her Love Song

Pocky
A Devil and Her Love Song
Song 18

National
TRAVELING ARROW SHOW
IT'S THE NATIONAL TRAVELING ARROW SHOW!
Shinichi Azumi
THIS WEEK WE'RE AT KOHAN MIDDLE SCHOOL IN OTSU CITY, SHIGA PREFECTURE!
WHAT COULD THAT AMAZING CONTRAPTION BE?
WE ENTER THE HUMAN BIRD CONTEST EVERY YEAR.
THIS IS OUR PILOT, OMI.
HELLO.
THIS IS THE RIGHT SHOW, ISN'T IT?
IT AIRED LAST NIGHT, SO I RECORDED IT.

You're so skinny!
I'm very light.
That's why you're the pilot.
Turn off when not in use.
MY DAD WATCHES IT TOO! HE'S USUALLY A REALLY UPTIGHT PRIEST...
...BUT HE'S ALL SMILES WHEN THIS IS ON.
MY MOM WATCHES THIS EVERY WEEK.
She works late, so she records it.
YOUR MOM DOES?!
BALD
Yusuke as a Buddhist priest
Yusuke Kanda's father...
Stare
TH-THMP
TH-THMP
W-what?!
HEY! ARE YOU ONLY HAVING ICE CREAM FOR LUNCH?
ENERGY JELLY
IT'S DELICIOUS. WANT SOME?
NO WAY.
EATING LIKE THAT'LL KILL YOU.

LOOK WHO'S TALKING! ALL YOU EAT IS PROTEIN JELLY, AND YOU'RE FREAKISHLY TALL! LIKE A BEANPOLE!
FREAK- -ISHLY?!
THIS IS HIGHLY NUTRITIOUS, I'LL HAVE YOU KNOW!
ICE CREAM IS FULL OF CALCIUM! IT'S NUTRITIOUS TOO!
...
MARIA, SHIN...
YOU'RE A LOT ALIKE.
I AM NOTHING LIKE THIS WORRY WART!
DON'T YOU COMPARE ME TO THIS BRAT!

AW, YOU LOOK LIKE YOU'RE HAVING FUN.
I'M JEALOUS.
Shut up! What is wrong with you?
I...
I AM...
...HAVING FUN.
I'M SO HAPPY JUST TO BE WITH YOU GUYS.
Did you see her face? She was blushing.
Ah ha... She'll get mad if you don't stop.
THAT'S WHAT I REALLY WANTED TO SAY.
BUT I WAS TOO EMBARRASSED TO SAY IT OUT LOUD.

SO I JUST REPEATED IT OVER AND OVER TO MYSELF.
ZSSSSSH
ARE YOU SERIOUS, HANA?
WE SHOULDN'T CALL HER "DEVIL MARIA"?
WE SHOULD BE **NICE** TO HER?
YOU SHOULDN'T TALK BADLY ABOUT PEOPLE, AYU.
HANA!
DANGLE

YOU'RE ALL SO SWEET!
I COULDN'T STAND IT IF ANYONE THOUGHT BADLY OF YOU...
...WHEN MARIA'S THE EVIL ONE HERE.
THE TEACHER TOLD ME...
...THAT THE CHORAL COMPETITION...
...WILL BE TELEVISED.
SO LET'S SHOW THE SCHOOL...
...AND ALL OF JAPAN JUST HOW GRACIOUS WE ARE.

SHE'S ARROGANT AND VIOLENT AND REFUSES TO FIT IN.
NO WONDER NO ONE LIKES HER!
BUT **WE'LL** FORGIVE HER.
MARIA WILL CHANGE HER WAYS AND THANK US AS WE ALL SING TOGETHER.
SHE'LL BE SO GLAD WE MADE A PLACE FOR HER.
WHO LOOKS LIKE THE ANGEL THEN?

WHO DO YOU THINK EVERYONE WILL SIDE WITH?
RIGHT, AYU?
Oh
IT'S ALL GOOD!
Beam
B-BUT...
...I CAN'T SEE HER THANKING US...

FWIP
SHHH
SHUP
MARIA WILL BE SO ISOLATED ...
...SHE'LL HAVE NO CHOICE BUT TO TURN TO US.
1-C
Stand

HANA IBUKI!
DID YOU LEAVE THIS HERE?
HUH? YES.
I HEARD IT WAS YOURS, SO I RETURNED IT RIGHT AWAY.
I PUT IT IN YOUR DESK AT LUNCH.
BUT THE CROSS IS MISSING...

OH, NO! IT WAS THERE WHEN I RETURNED IT...!
BZZZ
WZZZ
MAYBE IT SLIPPED OFF THE CHAIN...
I SAW HER RETURN IT.
THE CROSS WAS THERE.
I'LL GO LOOK FOR IT!
HANA!
BUT YOU'RE NOT THE ONE WHO LOST IT.

IT'S STILL MY RESPONSI-BILITY. I HAVE TO FIND IT.
WE'LL HELP YOU.
LET'S ALL LOOK FOR IT.
SHUFFLE
SHUFFLE
...
I DON'T LIKE THIS.
Over there?
We looked here already.
Check the desks.
I KNOW SHE MEANS WELL...
SO WHY ...?
MARIA.

WHY DON'T I FEEL LIKE THANKING HER?
IN THIS RAIN?
YEP...
HANA'S OUTSIDE LOOKING FOR IT.
I'LL GO STOP HER.
YEAH.
I'LL GO WITH YOU.

SHUT
SLIDE
Choral Competition Booklet
HEY!
WHAT IS IT?
IT'S THE BOOKLET FOR THE SONG.
THERE'S WRITING IN IT.
The origins of
List of Useless People
They're horrible.
Tomoyo Kohsaka
LOOK AT WHAT I FOUND IN MARIA'S DESK...
ISN'T THIS MARIA'S WRITING?
It's the same as in our copies.
WHAT?!
IT SAYS, "LIST OF USELESS PEOPLE."

"THE TWO GIRLS IN THE ORCHESTRA."
"I CAN'T BELIEVE THEY LIKE MUSIC. THEY'RE HORRIBLE."
WHAT ...?
BLUSH
WHAT? LET ME SEE THAT.
MUTTER
"TOMOYO KOHSAKA."
"SHE CAN'T EVEN READ ENGLISH. STUPID AND TONE DEAF."
THAT'S HARSH!
"SHIN MEGURO."
"HE THINKS HE'S SO GOOD AT PIANO. SO ANNOYING."

LOOK INSIDE MARIA'S BAG.
THERE'S PROBABLY MORE!
EMPTY IT!
TUMBLE
TUMBLE
...
HUH?
SOME-THING FELL.
CLANK
HEY... THIS IS...

HANA IBUKI!
ZSSH
STOP LOOKING FOR IT.
BUT—
IT'S FINE, HONESTLY.
NO! I HAVE TO FIND IT.
I KNOW IT'S IMPORTANT TO YOU.
I SHOULD'VE RETURNED IT PERSONALLY.
BUT I'LL FIND IT FOR YOU.
KOFF

IS YOUR ASTHMA ACTING UP?
UH-HUH. THEY LET ME LEAVE THE HOSPITAL, BUT...
KOFF KOFF
IF A FRIEND IS IN NEED...
...I CAN'T JUST DO NOTHING!
THOSE WERE BEAUTIFUL WORDS.
SO WHY DO I ONLY HEAR MALICE?
AND WHY IS SHE...

...LOOKING AT HIM AS SHE SAYS THAT?
THIS WAS IN MARIA'S BAG.
WHAT THE ...?!
AND THIS BOOKLET...
GLANCE
I CAN'T SAY I'M SURPRISED.
ALTHOUGH I GUESS SOME OF YOU...
...MAY BE SHOCKED THAT SHE WAS TALKING CRAP ABOUT YOU.
RIGHT, SHIN?
YOU'D BETTER FACE REALITY AND—

IT SOUNDS TOO NICE.
GO AHEAD, ASK HER ABOUT ME.
SHE'LL SAY, "HE TRIES TO ACT COOL, BUT INSIDE HE'S AN INSECURE COWARD WITH AN ATTITUDE."
OR "STOP SHOWING OFF, YOU ARROGANT POSER!"
SHE LETS YOU HAVE IT WITH BOTH BARRELS.
He's so right.
ANYWAY...

THAT IDIOT ALWAYS TELLS PEOPLE WHAT SHE THINKS RIGHT TO THEIR FACES!
STOP LOOKING FOR IT.
THIS IS GETTING ON MY NERVES.
BUT...
BUT IT MEANS A LOT TO YOU, RIGHT?
WHAT MAKES YOU THINK SO?
WELL... IT LOOKS EXPENSIVE.

THAT CROSS WAS GIVEN TO ME BY THE NUN I ATTACKED.
THAT'S HOW I GOT EXPELLED.
HOW...
HOW CAN YOU BE SO CALM...
...WHEN YOU'VE LOST SOMETHING SO SPECIAL?
DON'T YOU THINK THAT'S WEIRD, YUSUKE?

WHY...
...ARE YOU SUDDENLY SAYING THAT MARIA LOST IT?

ARE YOU JUST PRETENDING TO LOOK FOR IT?
AND YOU KEEP TALKING TO ME, NOT HER.
WHAT DO YOU WANT ME TO THINK?
I...
I JUST...
I THOUGHT IT WAS STRANGE THAT MARIA DOESN'T CARE ABOUT SUCH A PRECIOUS KEEPSAKE.
I-I WAS LOOKING FOR IT BECAUSE...
...WE'RE FRIENDS...

WE'RE NOT FRIENDS.

A Devil and Her Love Song

Song 19
A Devil and Her Love Song

"WE'RE NOT FRIENDS."
SHAA

UM...
WHAT WAS THAT?
I'M SORRY, BUT...
...I JUST CAN'T BELIEVE MY EARS.
CAN YOU REPEAT THAT?
I SAID WE'RE NOT FRIENDS.
WHAT?
...

HOW CAN YOU SAY SOMETHING SO CRUEL?
I'VE BEEN SO KIND TO YOU!
WHY SHOULD YOU GET TO DECIDE IF WE'RE FRIENDS OR NOT?
WHY AM I THE ONE BEING REJECTED?
HANA!
THERE'S SOMETHING WRONG WITH YOU, MARIA!
I DON'T KNOW WHAT YOU HAVE AGAINST ME, BUT...

ZSSSH
..."FRIENDSHIP MEANS DOING YOUR BEST TO GET ALONG WITH PEOPLE YOU DON'T EVEN LIKE.
WHAT DO YOU THINK I'M TRYING TO DO?
HANA...
YOU SHOULDN'T TALK TO HER LIKE THAT!

I'M SORRY.
YOU REACHED OUT TO ME...
...AND I PUSHED YOU AWAY.
WOULDN'T IT BE WONDERFUL...
I COULDN'T JUST...
...OPEN MY HEART TO YOUR KINDNESS.
...IF WE COULD ALL TRUST EACH OTHER AND GET ALONG?

IF ONLY MY HEART WAS PURE.
THIS COULD HAVE ALL BEEN SO BEAUTIFUL.
I'M SO WRETCHED. I'M SORRY.
YOU'RE ABSOLUTELY RIGHT.
ZSSSH
SOME-ONE EVEN TRIED TO TEACH ME...
...HOW TO PUT A LOVELY SPIN ON THINGS SO I DON'T HURT PEOPLE.
AND YET...

...EVERY TIME YOU TRY TO DO SOMETHING NICE...
...ALL I SEE IS HOW TWISTED YOU ARE.
PIPE DOWN, WILL YOU? LET IT GO.
NO, I WON'T!
MARIA'S FOOLING YOU!

HAND-WRITING CAN BE FAKED.
UGH
WHY DON'T YOU BELIEVE ME?
HOW DO YOU EXPLAIN THIS, THEN?
It was in Maria's bag.
GLARE
SHE PROBABLY DROPPED IT.
OR MAYBE SOMEONE PUT IT THERE.
THE PEOPLE WHO ACTUALLY GOT DISSED DON'T CARE.
JUST DROP IT.
THEN LET'S GO OUT-SIDE...
...AND MAKE HER TELL US THE TRUTH!
YEAH. MOVE ON.
FINE.

WHAT I'M SAYING MIGHT BE HURTFUL.
ZSSH
AND MAYBE I'M BEING UNGRATE-FUL...
...WHEN I DON'T ACCEPT YOUR KIND GESTURES.
BUT THAT'S REALLY HOW I FEEL.
YOU—
YOU **ARE** UNGRATE-FUL.
AND YOU'RE HURTFUL TOO.

SAYING SUCH AWFUL THINGS!
I'D NEVER TALK LIKE THAT TO ANYONE!
IT'D MAKE THEM HATE ME!
BUT I GUESS YOU'RE OKAY WITH THAT.
IT DOESN'T BOTHER YOU AT ALL.
HANA...
MARIA DOESN'T WANT TO BE HATED.
SHE COULDN'T CARE LESS IF I HATE HER OR NOT.
DO YOU HAVE ANY EMOTIONS AT ALL?
NOW I KNOW WHY AYU CALLS YOU "DEVIL MARIA."

ONLY A DEVIL...
...WOULDN'T BE SCARED OF PEOPLE HATING HER!
HANA!
STAY OUT OF THIS, YUSUKE!
OF COURSE THAT SCARES ME.
...BECAUSE I'VE REFUSED TO IGNORE THE TRUTH...
BUT...
...I'VE FELT SO MUCH JOY...
...THAT I'VE WANTED TO CRY.

SINCE I'M A DEVIL...
...I CAN'T ACCEPT THE GOOD IN LIFE WITHOUT THE EVIL.
SAY IT NICE AND CLEAR, LIKE THE DEVIL YOU ARE.
AM I YOUR FRIEND, MARIA?
OH!
...
TELL ME ONE MORE TIME...
...AND I'LL ACCEPT IT.

YOU'RE NOT MY FRIEND.

GUYS ...?
THERE! DID YOU HEAR THAT?
THAT'S HOW SHE IS!
HANA'S THE ONLY ONE WHO'S BEEN NICE TO HER...
...AND DEVIL MARIA BETRAYS HER LIKE IT'S NOTHING!
Is that true?
She just said so.
MARIA ...
DID YOU KNOW THEY WERE THERE?
NEVER MIND, EVERYONE.

I UNDER-STAND NOW.
SMILE
NO MATTER WHAT HAPPENS, SHE'LL NEVER BE MY FRIEND.
NO MATTER HOW HARD I TRY, IT'LL NEVER WORK.
I KNOW WHEN TO QUIT.
SO WHY DON'T WE SPLIT UP...
...FOR THE CHORAL COMPETITION?
TAKE WHOEVER YOU WANT FOR YOUR LITTLE GROUP.

HANA, WAIT!
STOP
...
WE FOUND YOUR CROSS IN YOUR DESK.
WE NEVER SHOULD'VE EVEN LOOKED FOR IT!
TOSS
CLATTER
ZSSH

HEY...!
STOP, YUSUKE KANDA.
CLANK
TMP
TMP
WASN'T IT IN HER BAG, NOT HER DESK?
IT'S BEING WASHED AWAY!
WHERE DOES THIS DRAIN EMPTY OUT?
WE HAVE TO HURRY.
IT'S FINE.
BUT IT MEANT A LOT TO YOU!
WHY AREN'T YOU UPSET, MARIA?!

IDIOT.
SHE CAN'T GET UPSET BECAUSE YOU'RE SO UPSET, YUSUKE.
ZSSH
Nurse's Office
HANA SAID WE SHOULD SPLIT UP.
WHAT'S GOING TO HAPPEN?
IT'S NOT LIKE HER. SHE REALLY CARES ABOUT UNITY.

I'M STAYING OUT OF IT.
SQUEEZE
GETTING INVOLVED WON'T HELP.
IT'LL ONLY COMPLICATE THINGS FOR MARIA.
Not very sympa-thetic...
I GET IT, SHIN.
IT'S POINTLESS FOR ME TO GET MAD.

THAT'S RIGHT.
MARIA CAN SPEAK FOR HERSELF.
BOYS MEDDLING IN GIRLS' BUSINESS...
...NEVER LEADS ANYWHERE GOOD.
I KNOW! DAD COMPLAINED WHEN PARISHIONERS CAME TO HIM WITH PROBLEMS.
"EVEN A DOG AVOIDS FIGHTS BETWEEN MAN AND WIFE."
THAT'S COMPLETELY IRRELEVANT.
What?
GUYS SURE CAN BE SIMPLE.

MARIA, WHY DON'T YOU AND I FORM A BAND?
WE CAN DO A HEAVY METAL VERSION OF "AMAZING GRACE"!
Shout
NOT GOING TO HAPPEN.
I'LL TRY TALKING TO HER TOMORROW.
It'd be so cool if we had matching black leather jackets...

SHE AND THE COMPETITION ARE SEPARATE ISSUES.
WE SHOULDN'T LET OUR PERSONAL PROBLEMS AFFECT THE CLASS.
YOU STILL THINK WE SHOULD ALL SING TOGETHER?
YES.
ARE YOU OKAY ... MARIA? ...

IT TURNS OUT HAVING SOMEONE GET MAD FOR YOU IS KIND OF NICE.
SORRY, BUT I'M TAKING OFF NOW.
I HAVE TO GET MY UNIFORM DRY.
HEY!
TAKE THIS.
YOU NEED IT, RIGHT?
FWSSH
Nice toss...
Catch it, will you?

DEEP DOWN, I STILL HOPE...
...THAT HANA IBUKI AND I CAN MAKE AMENDS.
Sha
Sha
ACHOO!
MAYBE NOT NOW, BUT SOMEDAY...
AND MAYBE NOT AS FRIENDS, BUT IN SOME OTHER WAY...
KRSH
GLUB
GLUB
I GUESS IT'S GONE...

CLINK
CLINK
I WILL BELIEVE.
GLUB GLUB
THE THREE OF THEM...
...ALL TOLD ME TO BELIEVE IN MYSELF...
KOFF
...BECAUSE THEY BELIEVE IN ME.

THEY BELIEVE I CAN MAKE CHANGE HAPPEN.
KOFF
KOFF
HELLO, JAPAN!
IT'S THE TRAVELING ARROW SHOW!
Is that Shinichi Azumi?!
No way!
National TRAVELING ARROW SH
TODAY WE'VE HIT TOTSUKA HIGH IN YOKOHAMA!
MUTTER
It's Azumi...!

OH MY GOSH, A TV CREW!
I KNOW THAT SHOW!
Eeeee!
WE'RE HAVING A CHORAL COMPETITION SOON!
...
REALLY? MAYBE WE SHOULD CHECK IT OUT.
HERE WE GO.
SO WHO'S IN CHARGE OF CLASS 1-C?
I'M THE LEADER AND CONDUC-TOR.
MY NAME IS HANA IBUKI.

A Devil and Her Love Song

A Devil and
Her Love Song
Song 20

IT'S A BEAUTIFUL DAY.
Amazing Grace...
CLINK
WHAT WAS LOST HAS BEEN FOUND.
How sweet the sound...
CLASP
AND WHEN I GET TO SCHOOL...
...I'LL SEE MY GOOD FRIENDS.
...that saved a wretch...

EVERYTHING IS WONDERFUL.
...like me...
I KNOW WE UNDER-STAND EACH OTHER.
That booklet of Maria's was interesting.
Shape up, boss lady.
I KNOW THINGS CAN CHANGE, AS LONG AS I DON'T GIVE UP!
TROT
TROT
SO...

...I'D BETTER FACE THINGS HEAD ON, AS USUAL.
HUFF HUFF
DASH
SHE'S NO DIFFERENT.
SHE DIDN'T CHANGE YESTERDAY, BUT SHE MIGHT TODAY.
EXACTLY! ALL THIS TIME...

...I'VE BEEN FAR TOO PASSIVE WITH HANA IBUKI.
HUFF
HUFF
CHATTER
CHATTER
WHO'S SHE TALKING TO?
HUFF
HUFF
KOFF
WE'RE HAVING A CHORAL COMPETITION SOON!
REALLY?
OH, SHOOT.
I RAN TOO FAST. OW, MY THROAT...
KOFF
KOFF
SO WHO'S IN CHARGE...
...OF CLASS 1-C?

I'M THE LEADER AND CONDUCTOR.
MY NAME IS HANA IBUKI.
ALTHOUGH I'M ACTUALLY STANDING IN.
STANDING IN?
YES. SOMEONE ELSE WAS IN CHARGE ORIGINALLY.
BUT SHE... WELL, SHE DIDN'T REALLY LIKE ME.
AND SHE DIDN'T FIT IN.
IT DIDN'T SEEM LIKE SHE WAS ENJOYING IT...
...SO...

...I THOUGHT I'D MAKE THINGS EASIER FOR HER—
WRENCH
THAT'S NOT TRUE AT ALL, HANA IBUKI!
WOW! SHE'S GORGEOUS ...
EEP!
MARIA —!
I WAS FORCED INTO IT AT FIRST, BUT...
...I'M QUITE SERIOUS ABOUT THIS.
True!
EARNEST
BUT...
BUT I BROUGHT THE CLASS TOGETHER...
You're serious?!
AND YOU SAID YOU DIDN'T LIKE ME!
I SAID NO SUCH THING.
Um ...
BUT YOU SAID WE WEREN'T FRIENDS!

THAT'S FINE. WE CAN BE SOMETHING ELSE.
HUH ...?
LET'S SEE NOW... MAYBE "COMRADES"?
NO, THAT'S NOT IT.
"CLASSMATES"? NO, NOT THAT EITHER.
TRAVELING ARROW SHOW
HOW SHOULD I PUT IT? WE'RE NEVER GOING TO SEE EYE TO EYE...
...SO WE MAY AS WELL HAVE SOME FUN WITH IT.
SCOOT
SCOOT

FROZEN
TILT
OH! "FRENEMIES"! ♡
HOW DOES THAT SOUND?
WHAT'S GOING ON WITH YOU, MARIA?
"FRENEMIES"? THAT'S RIDICULOUS!
Yu-suke!
Devil Maria's attacking Hana!
YOU NEVER KNOW UNLESS YOU TRY.
WHY SHOULD I DO THAT?
WHAT ARE YOU UP TO?

I THINK IT WOULD BE SAD...
...IF WE HAD NO RELATIONSHIP AT ALL.
HATING EACH OTHER ISN'T THE END OF THE WORLD.
THE FACT THAT WE FEEL SOMETHING...
...IS AMAZING IN AND OF ITSELF.
FOR WHATEVER REASON, OUR PATHS HAVE CROSSED.
ANY EMOTION IS BETTER THAN NONE!

IN THAT SENSE, YOU AND I...
...HAVE STRONG FEELINGS FOR EACH OTHER.
Um...
But...
They're negative...
SCOOT
SCOOT
SCOOT
IT'S A WASTE TO LET THINGS END THIS WAY!
LET'S EXPLORE A NEW KIND OF RELATIONSHIP.
YOU'RE SO WEIRD, MARIA!
How so?
MARIA...
I mean it!
SHE'S PUTTING A LOVELY SPIN ON IT, ALL RIGHT.
IS SHE AN IDIOT?
I TOLD HER TO LEAVE THINGS BE.
RAGH
RAGH

WELL, WHAT CAN YOU DO?
MURMUR
MURMUR
I UNDERSTAND HOW MARIA FEELS...
...BUT SHE'S SO IN-YOUR-FACE ABOUT IT.
ACHOO!
SOME-ONE'S TALKING ABOUT ME...
Caught a cold?
IF THAT ALWAYS MADE YOU SNEEZE, YOU'D NEVER STOP.
ANYWAY...

REALLY?
SHE LOOKED SCARED OF YOU.
HANA DIDN'T UNDERSTAND WHAT YOU MEANT.
YOU WERE KIND OF LIKE JASON.
"JASON"?
HAVEN'T YOU HEARD OF HIM?
AN UNKILLABLE MONSTER...
TOMOYO...
I HATE TO BREAK IT TO YOU, BUT YOUR SIMILES SUCK.
REALLY?
GOOD MORNING!
LISTEN, EVERYBODY. THE TV CREW IS GOING TO FILM OUR REHEARSAL.

SO THOSE OF YOU IN MARIA'S CAMP...
...PLEASE FIND SOMEWHERE ELSE TO BE.
THAT MEANS THE THREE OF YOU AND SHIN.
HANA!
WHY? YUSUKE'S COOL...
...AND SHIN'S OUR ACCOM-PANIST...
NO, NOT EVEN YUSUKE. NOT IF HE'S ON MARIA'S SIDE.
THAT'S HOW THINGS ARE WHEN YOU'RE NOT FRIENDS.
...

HANA, WILL YOU PLEASE JUST STOP—?
STRIDE
TURN
GRAB
COME WITH ME.
I WANT TO TALK TO YOU IN PRIVATE.
WHAT?!
LET ME GO, MARIA!
IT'S ABOUT TIME...

...for us to have a nice, long, heart-to-heart chat.
GLINK
YOU MAKE IT SOUND TERRIFYING, MARIA.
IT'S KOHSAKA-STYLE.
HEY! I'M A HARD ROCKER, NOT A TERRORIST!
WAIT ...
WHAP
GET YOUR HANDS OFF ME!
I HAVE NOTHING TO SAY TO YOU!
HANA IBUKI.

STOP TRYING TO MAKE ME SOUND UNHAPPY.
FOR YOUR INFORMATION...
WAIT...
...I AM NOT TWO-FACED!
I KNOW YOU'RE NOT.
What's going on? Oh, it's that girl.
Should we be filming?
LIAR! WHEN I'M KIND, YOU SAY IT'S ALL FAKE!
YOU'RE ALWAYS TRYING TO MAKE ME LOOK BAD.

THAT'S WHY YUSUKE'S TREATING ME SO COLDLY—!
ARE WE GETTING SOUND ...?
HUFF
HUFF
KOFF
HACK
HUFF
HUFF
HUFF
WAIT.
KOFF
KOFF
KOFF

KOFF KOFF
HUFF HUFF...
ARE YOU ALL RIGHT?
KOFF
FLINCH
DON'T TOUCH ME...
KOFF
HUFF HUFF...
HUFF...
YOU REALLY CARE FOR YUSUKE KANDA, DON'T YOU?
WHAT NOW?
ARE YOU TRYING TO SMOOTH THINGS OVER?
KOFF
NO, I'M NOT.

CAN YOU REALLY CUT SOMEONE OFF JUST BECAUSE...
...THEY SIDED WITH THE ENEMY?

AND YOU...
...LIKE HIM, RIGHT?

I...I DON'T KNOW ANYMORE.

MARIA...
HAVE YOU EVER FALLEN FOR A CHILDHOOD FRIEND?
KOFF
THEY'RE NOT LIKE ORDINARY FRIENDS, YOU KNOW?
YOU FEEL CLOSER TO THEM SOMEHOW.
BUT RECENTLY, I FINALLY REALIZED...
...THAT THEY'RE JUST SOMEONE YOU'VE KNOWN SINCE YOU WERE A KID.
ABOUT YUSUKE... THE THING IS...
...I SAW HIM ALL THE TIME WHEN WE VISITED THE FAMILY GRAVE.
KOFF KOFF
KOFF
Wanna rest?
BUT HE NEVER ONCE ASKED ME TO PLAY.
HE ONLY NOTICED ME WHEN I WAS SICK.

AND WHEN HE FINALLY SPOKE TO ME WHEN I **WASN'T** SICK...
...HE SAID, "GIVE ME BACK MARIA'S CROSS."
YUSUKE'S CRUEL.
HE'S NOT NICE AT ALL.
I THINK I'M OVER HIM NOW.
SO YOU'RE THE ONE WHO WROTE ALL THOSE MEAN THINGS IN MY BOOKLET.
YOU LEFT HIM OUT.
YOU COULDN'T BRING YOURSELF TO WRITE ABOUT HIM TOO.

THAT'S NOT—
YOU WERE PROBABLY TRYING TO BE NICE— TO BE LIKE HIM.
EVEN TO ME.
YOU SWALLOWED YOUR TRUE FEELINGS AND TRIED TO BE KIND.
THAT'S WHY YOU WERE STRUGGLING.
IT'S ALL RIGHT IF YOU DON'T LIKE ME.
NO MATTER WHAT YOU THINK OF ME OR HOW MUCH WE FIGHT...
...YUSUKE KANDA WON'T HATE YOU FOR IT.
AFTER ALL...

...YOU AND I ARE FRENEMIES.
YOU...
YOU'RE SUCH A KNOW-IT-ALL!
FINE! I'LL TELL YOU THE TRUTH.
THE TEACHERS WANT YOU ON TV AS THEIR POSTER GIRL...
...FOR HOW THE SCHOOL REFORMED A PROBLEM STUDENT WHO'D BEEN EXPELLED BEFORE.
THE POINT OF REHEARSING SEPARATELY WAS TO MAKE IT LOOK LIKE YOU DITCHED PRACTICE.

THEN AT THE END, I'D WELCOME YOU BACK...
...AND EVERYONE WOULD BE IMPRESSED BY HOW SWEET I WAS!
SO THAT WAS THE PLAN, HM?
...
OKAY.
That's easy enough.
Let's do it.

Continued
in
volume 4

YOU'RE SHIN MEGURO, RIGHT?
HOW ABOUT...
...I JUST CALL YOU "SHIN"?
HUH?!
DO I LOOK LIKE I WANT TO HEAR YOU CALL MY NAME?
♥DAY 3

...
UH-OH... I GUESS HE DOESN'T LIKE PEOPLE GETTING TOO FAMILIAR.
STOMP
STOMP
DAY 3
A Devil and Her Love Song Bonus Chapter
IT'S MY THIRD DAY OF HIGH SCHOOL.
HEY, YUSUKE!
I'VE BEEN GETTING ALONG WITH JUST ABOUT EVERYONE IN CLASS.

EVERYONE BUT HIM.
SNOOZE
WHAT WAS HIS NAME? SHIN MEGURO?
HE SURE STANDS OUT.
HE'S GOT A "DON'T TALK TO ME!" VIBE.
WHICH SCHOOL IS HE FROM?
It's all crumpled...
I THINK HE STUDIED ABROAD.
HE DODGED THE ENTRANCE EXAM.

BUT WE'RE ALL LIKE THAT, REALLY.
Oh, yeah.
ONE OF THOSE GUYS WHO DOESN'T CARE ABOUT ANYONE ELSE.
HE'S COLD.
WE ALL WANT TO HAVE FUN IN THE MOMENT.
BEING PERCEPTIVE DOESN'T MAKE YOU NICE.

1-C
I MAY BE COLD, TOO.
I GUESS MAYBE WE HAVE THAT IN COMMON.
Just heading in
Just heading out
I NEED A COUPLE OF VOLUNTEERS.
CAN YOU TWO SORT THESE PRINTOUTS AFTER CLASS?

SILENCE
FW
FW
FW
SO AWKWARD...
UM...
YOU CAN GO. I'LL FINISH UP.
FINE.
TURN

SLAM
HE ACTUALLY LEFT.
Ouch.
SO I HAVE TO FINISH ALL THIS BY MYSELF...
Ha... ha.
BUT AT LEAST I DON'T FEEL SO AWKWARD NOW.
HE SEEMS SO INSENSITIVE. HE PROBABLY DIDN'T EVEN NOTICE.
UM...
HEY!
AREN'T YOU LEAVING?
SLIDE

IN CASE YOU CAN'T HANDLE IT BY YOURSELF.
I'M ON STANDBY.
Ha ha
ACTUALLY, CAN YOU HELP ME...
... SHIN?
THAT WAS FAST ...
OH, WELL. I CAN'T HELP IT IF I WANT TO BE HIS FRIEND.
FROM NOW ON I'LL KEEP USING HIS NAME.
Fin

Greetings
JINGLE BELLS...
JINGLE ALL THE...
WOOOOOOO
JINGLE BELLS...
THANK YOU FOR READING A DEVIL AND HER LOVE SONG VOLUME 3!
I'M MIYOSHI TOMORI, AND I ABSOLUTELY CANNOT LIVE WITHOUT WARM BOTTLED DRINKS.
That's Tomori, not Momomori.
...WAY...
JINGLE JANGLE
THE OTHER DAY, THEY CAME OUT WITH "WARM NATURAL SPRING WATER." I WAS ECSTATIC. MAYBE IT'S JUST HOT WATER, BUT IF IT IS, IT'S CRYING OUT FOR A TEABAG!
I'VE TRIED ALL KINDS FROM CONVENIENCE STORES AND VENDING MACHINES.
Soba Tea
Kelp Tea
Healthy Green Tea
Sesame Tea
Flavan Tea
Brown Rice Tea
Raw Tea 1.5
Gokusen Tea
Jasmine Tea
Black Oolong Tea
Oi Tea Strong Taste
Izaamon
Warm Natural Mineral Water
Oi Tea
Leaf Tea
Soukenbi Tea Warm
STEAM
STEAM
STEAM
STEAM
ACTUALLY, I'M A TEA FREAK.
I REALLY PREFER STEEPING MY OWN TEA LEAVES, BUT ONE DAY, I BOUGHT WARM TEA IN A BOTTLE...
I EVEN BLEND MY OWN TEAS SOMETIMES.
...AND IT WAS SURPRISINGLY GOOD.
NOW I'M ADDICTED!

...EVERY PRODUCT THAT I'M ADDICTED TO GETS DISCONTINUED FOR SOME REASON.

McDonald's Pineapple Burger and Bacon Potato Pie

The Udon, Soba and Ramen Noodle Corner at Kappa Sushi

The Basil Tomato Rice Bowl at Sukiya

Instantly addictive Ramen Noodles

MIYOSHI

井吹ハナ
HANA IBUKI
Height: 150 cm
Likes sweaters, accessories, and knitted stuffed animals. She has naturally curly hair. She's a parishioner at Yusuke's temple, but isn't a Buddhist.
She looks skinny but is actually plump. But she's flat-chested...
Her family's grave is at his temple, but she visits a shrine for New Year's, celebrates Christmas, and wears a cross.

安積真一
SHINICHI AZUMI
Program Director + Host. Gay. A narcissist.
Traveling Arrow Crew
Sound man on left, cameraman on right. These three always travel together. They love to drink and often go to pubs after work. When he's drunk, Azumi often says "The 'Shin' in 'Shinichi' stands for 'truth'!"
RELAXING CHINESE NOODLES

I caught a cold on New Year's Eve. It'd been several years since I had the flu, and my temperature went up to nearly 104 degrees. I couldn't think at all and greeted the new year sleeping round-the-clock, hoping groggily that I would feel better the next time I opened my eyes. But I would wake up only to find that my fever hadn't broken. This cycle repeated over and over again, and before I knew it, New Year's Day and winter vacation had passed. I'm completely recovered from my bout with the flu now, but I'm troubled that it just doesn't feel like a new year to me.

-Miyoshi Tomori

Miyoshi Tomori made her debut as a manga creator in 2001, and her previous titles include *Hatsukare* (First Boyfriend), *Tongari Root* (Square Root), and *Brass Love!!* In her spare time she likes listening to music in the bath and playing musical instruments.

A DEVIL AND HER LOVE SONG

Volume 3

Shojo Beat Edition

STORY AND ART BY
MIYOSHI TOMORI

English Adaptation/Ysabet MacFarlane
Translation/JN Productions
Touch-up Art & Lettering/Monalisa de Asis
Design/Yukiko Whitley
Editor/Amy Yu

Printed in the U.S.A.

Published by VIZ Media, LLC
P.O. Box 77010
San Francisco, CA 94107

10 9 8 7 6 5 4 3 2 1
First printing, June 2012

www.viz.com www.shojobeat.com